Insect Repellents:

Top 20 Non-Toxic and Natural Repellent Recipes to Keep Away Mosquitoes, Flies, Spiders, Ants and Bugs

Table of content

Introduction

Let's be honest, most of the natural remedies out there don't work. That's what makes this guide different. What we've done is some basic research into what actually works, filtered through the fluff, the lies, the anecdotes to find the remedies that are backed by hard evidence. You will first be presented with some basic knowledge comparing chemicals commonly used with those that make up the essential components of the recipes used for the repelling different types of bugs and pests in conjunction with the science of both. Then we will give you well researched tips and tricks on things you can do to maximize your war on bugs. While most artificial chemicals and repellants are more effective in certain situations, there are still components you can find that are natural, inexpensive, and simple to put together. This is where things get interesting. We'll provide you with twenty different recipes that you can easily put together to keep away pesky critters without breaking your wallet. We'll even give you optional ingredients that you can choose from to add to your recipes to make them more effective and beneficial to your skin, if applying them topically, or to the air, if you are applying them on a surface. Keep reading.

Chapter 1 – Tips and Tricks

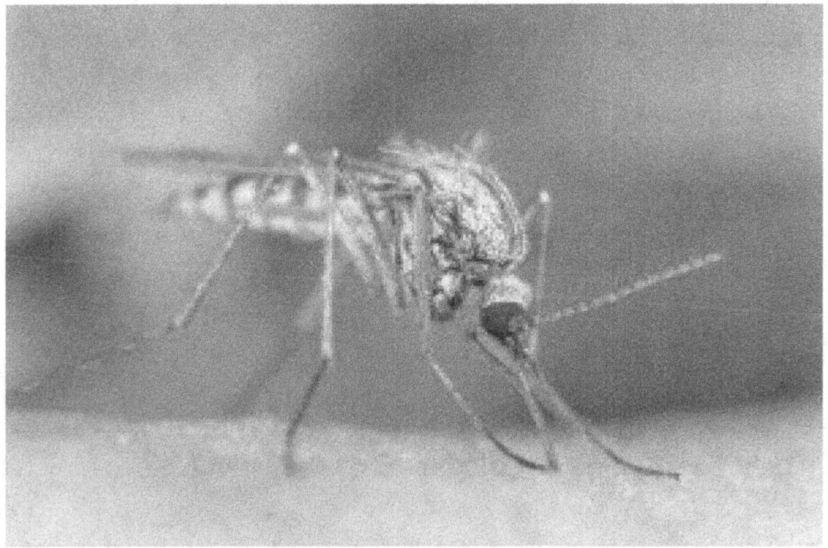

Before you begin making your bug repellants, you want to make sure that you have eliminated as much of the behaviors that attract bugs in the first place. This starts by cleaning up. Clean up the inside and outside of your home, your car, and your yard. Get rid of standing water, clutter, exposed food, waste, and anything else that is not essential to the décor of your home. Next, you want to inspect your home for places and entry points where insects may be arriving. Plug up holes, use adequate insulation, and inspect screen doors. In addition, you should always thoroughly inspect used furniture or decorations before you bring them into your home. Make sure there is no evidence of bug droppings, eggs, termites, roaches, or other suspicious holes. It may be difficult to weed out all suspicious items, but the general rule should be that if you are unsure or in doubt about an item, it's best to leave it alone and let it go.

It goes without saying that if you leave your home you have limited control over the factors that attract insects, and if you are an outdoors person, the only control you may have is the clothes you wear and what you put on over your skin. As a result, familiarize yourself with the insects in your area and what attracts them. Wear appropriate clothing. Obviously you can't completely cover your skin if you are going to engage in strenuous physical activity or travel to a hot destination. In those instances, be aware of your surroundings, and be meticulous with the scents and odors your use. If you are pregnant or in a sensitive health group, you should consider forgoing travel or excursions to places that put you at enhanced risk.

Another note of recommendation is to use the recipes that work best for you. There are several choices for your repellant, so if you find that one recipe doesn't work as well as you like or if you have a reaction to the repellant or dislike the smell, try another one of the options. Everyone has different things that impact them differently, things like genetics, allergies, health conditions, and other factors. Find what works best for you, and then run with it.

If you choose to ignore the suggestions in this section, don't be surprised if you still find that you have a bug problem. If you hate flies and you've tried all the different fly options, but you also decide not to clean up the dog excrement in your back yard or frequently clean the cat litter in your home, don't be surprised if the flies stick around. Use common sense, and take an all of the above approach to eliminating your bug problem. You may not get rid of 100% of all bugs, but you will at least make progress and improve upon your current situation.

Chapter 2 – Eliminating Mosquitoes

Eliminating standing water is key. Make sure you do this first. If you're going to be in an area with standing water in your travels, cover your skin as much as possible. Also, limit scented perfumes and moisturizers. If you are in a region at high risk for malaria or other mosquito borne illnesses, use a mosquito net at night, and make sure that ventilated areas are covered with screens. Also, most but not all mosquitoes (such as the Aedes mosquitoes which carry Zika and are active during the day) are most active in the hours around sunrise and sunset. Minimizing skin exposure and using filters and netting during these times will have the greatest impact.

Deet used to be the single most effective ingredient in store bought mosquito repellents. It's long lasting and effective. It used to be the most effective option available. There are some warnings, however, mainly for pregnant women, woman that are breastfeeding, infants, or those in certain groups. In addition, chemicals at concentrations of 30% Deet or higher have been linked to certain conditions such as rashes, seizers, and other complications.

A new chemical, Picaridin, developed by Bayer, works by mimicking components of pepper and makes the skin less desirable for mosquitoes to attack. Studies recently show that it matches the effectiveness of Deet, but it does so in lower concentrations with similar duration, no smell, and no known side effects. Still, it is a relatively new chemical, and some people may have concerns related to unknown impacts based on the newness. Generally, concerns over safety after a product has been out for a decade should be enough to eliminate most concerns, and I would feel perfectly safe using the product. If, however, you still have concerns, then the natural recipes below may be a better option for your peace of mind.

Before getting into specific recipes, you should also be aware that many of the remedies and suggestions you may see on the internet do not work, so let's go through a few of them so you know what to avoid. First of all, the color of your clothing will have little impact on whether or not mosquitoes will bite it. While there is some evidence suggesting dark colors are used to hone in on the target, the main culprit is heat and carbon dioxide. Humans exhale enough carbon dioxide to make them a sitting target for mosquitoes, so much so, that when they have spotted you based on your breath, the color of jeans will do little to save you.

In addition, using plants, lamps, lights, candles, coils, or other external detractors will have little impact on you getting bitten. Mosquitoes will simply avoid the objects they don't like and move around them. Mosquito attractors, like buzz lamps and lights, will actually attract more mosquitoes than they kill leaving you with a worse problem than when you started. Industrial foggers and sprays are expensive, temporary, and defeat the whole purpose of this book.

Also, some commonly touted ingredients have shown limited effectiveness, so you shouldn't waste your time or money. Those include rosemary oil, geraniol, cinnamon oil, lemongrass, and cedar oils. You can view some of those studies by Consumer Reports here. A few oils do work, and we'll get to those in a moment.

Other remedies with limited or no effectiveness with possible hidden dangers (and this goes for their use against other types of insects as well) include, supplements of any kind, ultrasonic devices, and wristbands, so don't waste your money.

Now for the good stuff. Main ingredients that have been show to work through various trials and studies include lemon eucalyptus oil, Sichuan pepper (Zanthoxylum limonella) essential oil, lime (Citrus Aurantifolia) essential oil, as well as catnip oil (Neptalactone). Concentrations are most effective and longest lasting at 20%, but still hold some effectiveness as low as 5%.

In addition, some ingredients may be used to enhance the duration or effectiveness of those ingredients when used as a base and include mustard oil (the most effective) and coconut oil. A couple of other bases that can be added that don't enhance the effectiveness but do have other qualities such as healing or moisturizing properties include aloe vera and agave nectar. You can make adjustments with the existing repellant recipes below, just remember that the effectiveness is greatest at 20% and the mustard oil base is also the most effective enhancer. In addition, other ingredients not listed below may limit the effectiveness by cancelling out the impact of the main ingredient or by being an attractant through smell. With no further ado, the recipes are listed below.

Recipe #1

Lemon Eucalyptus Oil: Ingredients 100% Lemon Eucalyptus Oil .5 oz (10 mills), 100% Mustard oil base 2 oz. Instructions, add the ingredients together, stir, and pour into storage container for later use. Estimated cost: $9. **Caution:** Do not use if you have a known allergy to any ingredient. Test a small amount on a small section of your skin first before applying over to larger region. **Option 2:** Replace

Mustard oil with coconut oil as a base. **Option 3:** Replace place with either aloe vera or agave nectar depending on preference. Effectiveness and duration may be reduced, but the repellant will have less abrasiveness to the skin and enhances moisturizing properties. **Option 4:** In addition to implementing suggesting in either option 2 or 3, drop the concentrations of the Essential Oil to ¼ oz OR increase the base ingredient by a factor of 4. Keep in mind, reducing the concentration of the main ingredient to 5% reduced the effectiveness and limits the duration of the effectiveness.

Recipe #2

Sichuan Pepper (Zanthoxylum limonella) Essential Oil: Ingredients 100% Sichuan Pepper (Zanthoxylum limonella) 1 oz, 100% Mustard oil base 4 oz. Instructions, add the ingredients together, stir, and pour into storage container for later use. Estimated cost: $3. **Caution:** Do not use if you have a known allergy to any ingredient. Test a small amount on a small section of your skin first before applying over to larger region. **Option 2:** Replace Mustard oil with coconut oil as a base. **Option 3:** Replace place with either aloe vera or agave nectar depending on preference. Effectiveness and duration may be reduced, but the repellant will have less abrasiveness to the skin and enhances moisturizing properties. **Option 4:** In addition to implementing suggesting in either option 2 or 3, drop the concentrations of the Essential Oil to ¼ oz OR increase the base ingredient by a factor of 4. Keep in mind, reducing the concentration of the main ingredient to 5% reduced the effectiveness and limits the duration of the effectiveness.

Recipe #3

Lime (Citrus Aurantifolia) Essential Oil: Ingredients 100% Lime (Citrus Aurantifolia) Essential Oil .5 ounce (10 mills), 100% Mustard oil base 2 oz. Instructions, add the ingredients together, stir, and pour into storage container for later use. Estimated cost: $14. **Caution:** Do not use if you have a known allergy to any ingredient. Test a small amount on a small section of your skin first before applying over to larger region. **Option 2:** Replace Mustard oil with coconut oil as a base. **Option 3:** Replace place with either aloe vera or agave nectar depending on preference. Effectiveness and duration may be reduced, but the repellant will have less abrasiveness to the skin and enhances moisturizing properties. **Option 4:** In addition to implementing suggesting in either option 2 or 3, drop the concentrations of the Essential Oil to ¼ oz OR increase the base ingredient by a factor of 4. Keep in mind, reducing the concentration of the main ingredient to 5% reduced the effectiveness and limits the duration of the effectiveness.

Recipe #4

Catnip Oil (Neptalactone): Ingredients 100% Catnip Oil (Neptalactone) .2 ounce (4 mills), 100% Mustard oil base 1.8 oz. Instructions, add the ingredients together, stir, and pour into storage container for later use. Estimated cost: $17. **Caution:** Do not use if you have a known allergy to any ingredient. Test a small amount on a small section of your skin first before applying over to larger region. **Option 2:** Replace Mustard oil with coconut oil as a base. **Option 3:** Replace place with either aloe vera or agave nectar depending on preference. Effectiveness and duration may be reduced, but the repellant will have less abrasiveness to the skin and enhances moisturizing properties. **Option 4:** In addition to implementing suggesting in either option 2 or 3, drop the concentrations of the Essential Oil to ¼ oz OR increase the base ingredient by a factor of 4. Keep in mind, reducing the concentration of the main ingredient to 5% reduced the effectiveness and limits the duration of the effectiveness.

Chapter 3 – Those Pesky Flies

Flies come in all shapes and sizes. They are notorious for spreading various diseases based on their habits and living environments. Whether you are trying to get rid of bar flies, fruit flies, common house flies, or other varieties, there are a few things you should do first. The first thing is to make sure you thoroughly clean all surfaces, frequently throw away garbage and clean up any foul odor. You also need to cover all food and drinks, preferable with a non-permeable seal. It that's not possible, then you should refrigerate items that can't be properly sealed as well as consume foods such as pasta and rice as quickly as possible, making sure to throw away all expired foods.

The above steps focus on controlled the breeding environments and growth of flies. Following aforementioned steps alone should limit a significant portion of your fly problem at home or your target location, such as a bar or a restaurant. This is only one step, though, and if you already have an infestation, you will need to take additional measures. This includes finding any breading source or location.

The second step may be difficult or nearly impossible if you live in a densely populated area as they could be breading as far as 1,000 feet away. If are in a rural area, it may be possible to find the source, which could be things like open sewers, storm drains, fruit trees, or decomposing carcasses. Still, if you can get rid of any dead animals or eliminate decomposing matter it will help.

Once you've done your best to locate the source, target the flies you can see. I would use a good old fashioned fly swatter if they are big enough. It's old school, but it's effective to a degree. Once you've gotten as many as you can or you have enough energy to kill, the next step is to employ the tried and true method of fly paper. The good news is that you don't have to use just any old fly paper or even buy it from the store. There are several simple ways you can make your own fly paper in just about any color.

Recipe #5

Flypaper #1: Supplies & ingredients: 2" to 3" wide paper strips, string, white or brown sugar, honey, water, a pot, and a bowl. Instructions: Cut your paper strips. You can use any type or color of paper you prefer. Punch a hole into the paper, and then loop the string, and make a knot so you can tie or hang the paper in the location of your choice. Alternatively, you can decide to purchase tape, and then apply to homemade flypaper to the tape at the location of your choice. Next, melt the sugar or brown sugar along with honey and water in a small sauce pan until the sugar melts and dissolves in low heat. Pour the mixture into a small bowl, then dip the strips in the mixture taking care to make sure that they are completely covered. Once completed, you are free to hang the strips or attach them to adhesive surfaces at the location of your choice.

Recipe #6

Flypaper #2: Supplies & ingredients: 2" to 3" wide paper strips, string, white or brown sugar, molasses, water, a pot, and a bowl. Instructions: Cut your paper strips. You can use any type or color of paper you prefer. Punch a hole into the paper, and then loop the string, and make a knot so you can tie or hang the paper in the location of your choice. Alternatively, you can decide to purchase tape, and then apply to homemade flypaper to the tape at the location of your choice. Next, melt the sugar or brown sugar along with molasses and water in a small sauce pan until the sugar melts and dissolves in low heat. Pour the mixture into a small bowl, then dip the strips in the mixture taking care to make sure that they are completely covered. Once completed, you are free to hang the strips or attach them to adhesive surfaces at the location of your choice.

Recipe #7

Flypaper #3: Supplies & ingredients: 2" to 3" wide paper strips, string, white or brown sugar, corn syrup, apple juice, a pot, and a bowl. Instructions: Cut your paper strips. You can use any type or color of paper you prefer. Punch a hole into the paper, and then loop the string, and make a knot so you can tie or hang the paper in the location of your choice. Alternatively, you can decide to purchase tape, and then apply to homemade flypaper to the tape at the location of your choice. Next, melt the sugar or brown sugar along with corn syrup & apple juice in a small sauce pan until the sugar melts and dissolves in low heat. Pour the mixture into a small bowl, then dip the strips in the mixture taking care to make sure that they are completely covered. Once completed, you are free to hang the strips or attach them to adhesive surfaces at the location of your choice.

Recipe #8

Flypaper #4: Supplies & ingredients: 2" to 3" wide paper strips, string, white or brown sugar, pancake syrup, flavored tea, a teapot, and a bowl. Instructions: Cut your paper strips. You can use any type or color of paper you prefer. Punch a hole into the paper, and then loop the string, and make a knot so you can tie or hang the paper in the location of your choice. Alternatively, you can decide to purchase tape, and then apply to homemade flypaper to the tape at the location of your choice. Next, prepare the tea with the flavor and scent of your choice, then melt the sugar or brown sugar along with pancake syrup & heated tea in a a small bowl, then dip the strips in the mixture taking care to make sure that they are completely covered. Once completed, you are free to hang the strips or attach them to adhesive surfaces at the location of your choice.

Chapter 4 – Scare Away the Eight-Legged Crawlers

Spiders can give you the frights, but not all spiders are bad. They eat many other bugs, so you may want to be careful with exactly which spiders kill and where you kill your spiders. Of course, many spiders are poisonous, and the ones that are not can still pack a nasty bite if they are caught off guard, so first here are a few tips.

Make sure you carefully inspect only shoes and dark places prior to diving in. You can tap on your shoes with the opening facing the bottom first to shake out any of the critters. Also, if you are trying to get at dusty cobwebs that may still contain live spiders and eggs, use a long stick or broom to reach and swat away any of the spiders keeping the creatures as a substantial distance and away from your skin. When clearing out spiders, you should also be covered, with your socks folded over your pants and wearing gloves to cover your hands over long sleeves. Also, use a flashlight and as much lighting as possible prior to entering dark spaces. Open drawers or doors with a tool, broom, or stick prior to entering to avoid jumping spiders. Once you've taken precautions and cleared out what you can, make sure that you have properly sealed up any cracks or holes.

Recipe #9

Lemon Eucalyptus Oil: Ingredients 100% Lemon Eucalyptus Oil (5 mills), ½ cup of lime concentrate. ½ cup of water. Instructions, add the ingredients together, stir, and pour into spray bottle. Spray into cracks, crevices, and dark areas where spiders have been known to lurk. Estimated cost: $5.

Recipe #10

Lemon Eucalyptus Oil: Ingredients 100% Lemon Eucalyptus Oil (5 mills), ½ cup of lemon concentrate. ½ cup of water. Instructions, add the ingredients together, stir, and pour into spray bottle. Spray into cracks, crevices, and dark areas where spiders have been known to lurk. Estimated cost: $5.

Recipe #11

Lemon Eucalyptus Oil: Ingredients 100% Lemon Eucalyptus Oil (5 mills), 1 tablespoon of grapefruit juice. ½ cup of water. Instructions, add the ingredients together, stir, and pour into spray bottle. Spray into cracks, crevices, and dark areas where spiders have been known to lurk. Estimated cost: $5.

Recipe #12

Lemon Eucalyptus Oil: Ingredients 100% Lemon Eucalyptus Oil (5 mills), 1 3 tablespoons of salt, 1 cup of water. Instructions, add the ingredients together, stir, and pour into spray bottle. Spray into cracks, crevices, and dark areas where spiders have been known to lurk. Estimated cost: $5.

Chapter 5 – Effective Ant Solutions

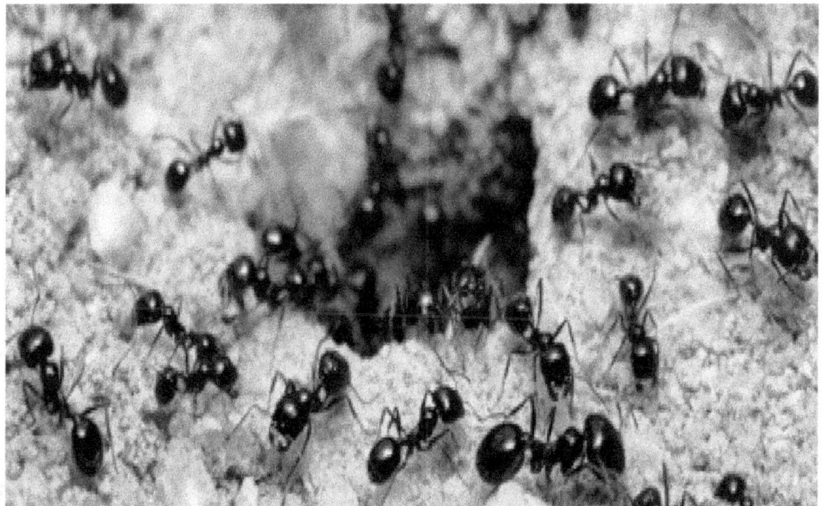

As with spiders, ants can be beneficial and kill other insects and pests. Still, they can be pests themselves as well as cause painful bites depending on the variety. The first step in getting rid of ants is cleaning up any food or crumbs. Make sure you seal up all food containers, you wash dishes quickly, and you throw away any garbage with food scraps as soon as possible. Also, make sure you wipe down the sink area and add water and turn on the dish disposal for a few seconds after using it to clear out any food below. Next, you want to plug up any holes. Follow the ant trail if you see any, and the use permanent sealant or find some other way to seal off the openings you find.

Once you've done the basics there are a few things you can do to kill ants on your own. Start with the basics first. You can take a wet sponge and then wipe down the ant trail and rinse the sponge off in the sink. If you locate an ant hill with a nest, you can kill off most of the ants in the nest by pouring down a pot of boiling water over the nest. If the ants are coming in from another source, you should use some of the recipes below.

Recipe #13

Borax #1: Ingredients 100% Borax powder, 1 tablespoon of peanut butter. Instructions, lay down the peanut butter on a flat surface where ants have been known to congregate. Next, spread a thick line of borax about 1-inch-thick completely surrounding the peanut butter in a circle. Estimated cost: $2.

Recipe #14

Borax #2: Ingredients 100% Borax powder, 1 tablespoon of white sugar. Instructions, lay down the white sugar on a flat surface where ants have been known to congregate. Next, spread a thick line of borax about 1-inch-thick completely surrounding the peanut butter in a circle. Estimated cost: $2.

Recipe #15

Boric Acid #1: Ingredients 100% Boric Acid, 1 tablespoon of peanut butter. Instructions, lay down the peanut butter on a flat surface where ants have been known to congregate. Next, spread a thick line of Boric Acid about 1-inch-thick completely surrounding the peanut butter in a circle. Estimated cost: $2.

Recipe #16

Boric Acid #2: Ingredients 100% Boric Acid, 1 tablespoon of white sugar. Instructions, lay down the white sugar on a flat surface where ants have been known to congregate. Next, spread a thick line of Boric Acid about 1-inch-thick completely surrounding the peanut butter in a circle. Estimated cost: $2.

Chapter 6 – Other Bug Repellants and Solutions

Roaches

As with, ants, the first step in getting rid of ants is cleaning up any food or crumbs. Make sure you seal up all food containers, you wash dishes quickly, and you throw away any garbage with food scraps as soon as possible. Also, make sure you wipe down the sink area and add water and turn on the dish disposal for a few seconds after using it to clear out any food below. Remove any standing water to take away the roaches water supply. Also, make sure that you always wash and dry any used clothes prior to bringing them in your home, and clean out any suitcases or storage containers to make sure there are no roaches or roach eggs.

Before you get started, you should also be aware that roaches do not care about citrus or just about any other essential oil. Most natural remedies will not work against these pests so your options will be limited to a few steps. The first is removing their food source, manual collection through traps and strips is another option, and finally, killing through natural bug poisons such as borax and boric acid. The latter is the best solution, though you should also employ the first step for general maintenance. You many also want to use traps initially, just for your own peace of mind when you are first tackling the problem.

Recipe #17

Boric Acid: Ingredients 100% Boric Acid. Instructions, spread lines of boric acid is as many cracks and crevices as possible. Spread them on the edges of corners on the floor and table top surface corners. The bugs will die over time due to prolonged exposure. Optional: Place sugary foods or peanut butter in the center of completely enclosed circle of the powder, though, this is not necessary. **Caution:** Avoid prolonged exposure to the skin, and avoid spreading on surfaces where small children crawl. Estimated cost: $2.

Recipe #18

Borax: Ingredients 100% Borax. Instructions, spread lines of boric acid is as many cracks and crevices as possible. Spread them on the edges of corners on the floor and table top surface corners. The bugs will die over time due to prolonged exposure. Optional: Place sugary foods or peanut butter in the center of completely enclosed circle of the powder, though, this is not necessary. **Caution:** Avoid prolonged exposure to the skin, and avoid spreading on surfaces where small children crawl. Estimated cost: $2.

Recipe #19

Baits: Ingredients Any sugary food or peanut butter, adhesive strips, small container or box. Instructions, lay down the adhesive strips. Next, spread the food over the adhesive strips, making sure there is at least two to three inches of width surrounding the food. Replace and repeat as needed. Estimated cost: $1.

Bed Bugs

Bed bugs are making a comeback for a variety of reasons. While they don't spread disease, they do leave nasty marks. For prevention, make sure that you always wash and dry any used clothes prior to bringing them in your home, and clean out any suitcases or storage containers. Also, I would inspect carefully any used furniture before you bring it in your home. I also don't recommend buying used mattresses unless it from a well-respected store or a source that you trust. Assuming that you've already found an infestation, the first thing you will need to do is to wash and dry all clothing and linens. In fact, I would recommend completely destroying bed sheets and spreads.

Next, it's time to kill these suckers. There is really only one way to kill bed bugs naturally, heat. Don't waste your money on sprays and other natural remedies. Trust me on this one. You will end up wasting your money and end up no closer to solving your problem. I would also recommend that you look up some online video tutorials prior to using the heat solution just to be doubly sure that you did the job, safely and effectively. First all, don't use a hair dryer! It is nearly impossible to regulate the amount of heat you need, and it's not safe as you are likely to burn areas of your bed or mattress and might even cause a fire, so just don't it!

Recipe #20

Heat: Vacuum, Steam Cleaner, large black garbage bags. Instructions: Wash all clothes and linens in hot water and heat dry all clothes and linens for at least 30 minutes. Next, vacuum thoroughly around the mattress and bed frame as well as any pillows and furniture. Steam clean using a good steam cleaner your mattress, pillow, and any furniture cushions as well as your fabric curtains and rugs. Finally, place any pillows or cushions in a large black garbage bag, careful not to overstuff the bags. Lay the bag out as flat as possible in the hot sun so the heat gets trapped in the bags. Leave the bags out beginning late morning, and then remove them about an hour before the sun rises if the temperature is at least 70 degrees F outside. Estimated cost: Varies.

Conclusion

Now that you've been thoroughly versed with your natural remedies and options, the ball is in your court. Remember that if you are serious about your bug problems, you have to attack the problem with fidelity, in other words, be consistent. Start with the basics by eliminating the things that attract bugs in the first place, and be mindful of the behaviors that put you at risk. Keep your eyes open for warning signs of bug activity, and then throw down the gauntlet by using an all of the above approach. Remove clutter and attractors, wear appropriate clothing, eliminate bug magnets, and then top it off with the repellants best suited for your situations.

FREE Bonus Reminder

If you have not grabbed it yet, please go ahead and download your special bonus report *"Leptin Resistance. 21 Leptin Recipes For Weight Loss & Healthy Living"*.

Simply Click the Button Below

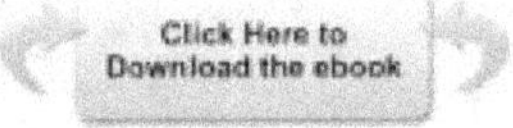

OR **Go to This Page**

http://easyweightlossway.com/free/

BONUS #2: More Free & Discounted Books

Do you want to receive more Free & Discounted Books?

We have a mailing list where we send out our new Books when they go free or with a discount on Kindle. Click on the link below to sign up for Free & Discount Book Promotions.

=> Sign Up for Free & Discount Book Promotions <=

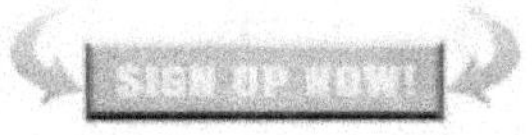

OR Go to this URL